THE
STORY
of GOD
Our KING

Written by
KENNETH PADGETT
& SHAY GREGORIE

Illustrated by
AEDAN PETERSON

Wolfbane
BOOKS

KENNETH PADGETT and his wife, Rebecca, live in the South Carolina Lowcountry with their two young daughters. Kenneth is a PhD (cand) in Biblical Studies at Trinity College, Bristol (UK), and serves in his local church as the Scholar-In-Residence. He also holds a Master's degree in Old Testament from Gordon-Conwell Theological Seminary. Sitting in a deer stand with a good book and a pipe is his happy place.

SHAY GREGORIE is a native of Mount Pleasant, South Carolina, where he lives with his wife, Catherine, and their eight children. He holds a Master of Divinity degree from Gordon-Conwell Theological Seminary, is a business owner, and an ordained pastor in the Anglican Church of North America. His favorite thing to do with his kids is late-night flounder gigging, for which he employs Mexican Coke (made with real sugar) and watermelon Sour Patch Kids to stay awake.

AEDAN PETERSON is an illustrator and visual developer born and raised in Nashville, Tennessee. He's been busy for the last few years, illustrating the new edition of *Pembrick's Creaturepedia*, *The Tree Street Kids* books, and *Dead-eye Dan and the Cimarron Kid*. He's also delved into the world of animation working as a character designer and background artist for *The Wingfeather Saga* animated series. When he's not drawing, he can often be found bird watching, or eating chips and salsa, or doing both at the same time.

Copyright © 2022 by Wolfbane Books

Published by
Wolfbane Books
1164 Porcher's Bluff Road
Mount Pleasant, SC 29466
www.wolfbanebooks.com

Cover and interior illustrations by Aedan Peterson
Cover and interior design by Brannon McAllister

Hardcover edition ISBN: 978-1-7366106-2-6
First Edition

Printed in China
10 9 8 7 6 5 4 3 2 1

For my father, who has been showing me what being a
defender and friend looks like my whole life.

—KENNETH

For my dad, who bows his knee to The King. Thanks
for showing me what a faithful father looks like.

—SHAY

To Pops, thanks for being a downright great dad and for
always reminding me that the stories are true.

—AEDAN

Most stories about kings involve epic battles
against evil enemies in order to save a kingdom.
But these are mere shadows of the true story of the
whole world.

Our world has a King, a Kingdom, and a royal
story that's still unfolding today!

If you're wondering where the Kingdom is, look
around you. If you're wondering who the King is,
keep watch, and listen closely. He wants you to
know Him, because He already knows you.

He's a King like no other,
  defender and friend.
Always and forever,
  world without end!

In the very beginning, before there was anything, even in the darkness, our King reigned supreme. Water and waves rumbled in the wild and waste. And like the light of seventy suns, the King's words lit up the universe!

He spoke and the earth burst forth towering trees,
The sky started buzzing with birds, bugs, and bees,
Schooling things of all sizes swam the bright blue seas!

So much light and so much life flowed from the heart of the King.
Then He prepared His Kingdom for the very best thing!
He created people who could love, laugh, and sing.

Would His Kingdom last forever? Could it even get any better?

The very next day the King rested on His throne, and gave
His people loving laws that set them free to flourish in the
garden. He wanted them to fill the earth with a great big
royal family!

Adam was the first husband of the first wife,
and Eve was the mother of all life.

God created them to rule and reign over the earth with Him,
to share His dominion in a world without end!

What kind of king does that? Could it even be true?
That He would share His rule with me and with you?

He's a King like no other,
  defender and friend.
Always and forever,
  world without end!

But you'll never guess what happened next!

A creature full of hate—a scaly beast, radiant and awful—
slithered through the shadows of the garden!

And in the saddest moment there ever was, he convinced
Adam and Eve to turn away from their good King, and hand
over the great gift God had given them.

Before things got better, they got worse…so much worse!

Death and darkness overwhelmed the world God had made.

So He washed it with wild rumbling waters that spread clear across the land.

It seemed like the Serpent-King had destroyed the good King's plan!

But those who knew God knew better.

All creation was eagerly waiting. A hush fell over the King's army of angels. The stars and planets hovered with hope.

And without any warning, in a faraway land, the King appeared to a man called Abraham.

God revealed a plan for a royal Son!
Soon the Serpent-King would be undone!

He'll be a King like no other,
defender and friend.
Always and forever,
world without end!

For a long, long time, Abraham's family grew and flourished.

Then one day an evil king became worried that they would grow to be a kingdom greater than his own. So he made them slaves, to build his kingdom—out of dry dusty stone!

It was one of the darkest times ever for God's people, and the land was flooded with sorrow.

But their good King heard their cries. He stretched
out His right hand and destroyed the enemy with
the unstoppable fury of a determined Father.
Rushing waters rumbled and roared - over, under,
and through God's enemies!

God would never let His people be taken.
He promised to never, ever leave or forsake them!

He's a King like no other,
  defender and friend.
Always and forever,
  world without end!

Through the waters, and across the wild, God carried His royal family. Together they could be a blessing to the whole world! But, as you might expect by now, another evil enemy slithered across their path…a fierce giant who threatened to wipe out God's family.

But while death was looming over them, a small boy named David remembered the mighty acts of their Great King of Old, how He had tossed the Serpent-King into the rumbling waters…

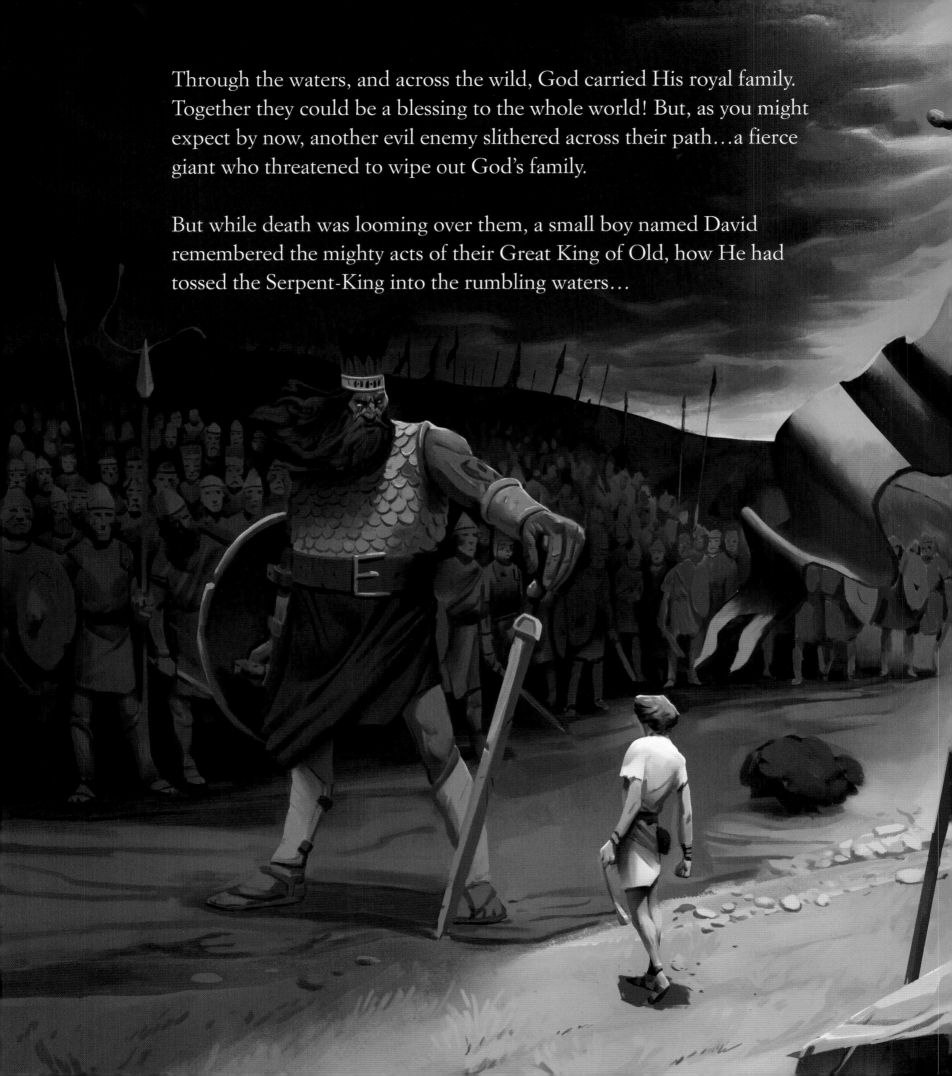

And young David himself slayed the scaly beast!
He went on to rule as king through years of war and peace.

Could David be the Forever-King—the long-awaited, promised Son?

There's still more story to unfold before we meet the chosen One.

The Great King of Old had a plan and a promise. The plan was too wonderful—even for King David to fulfill—but the promise was perfect!

Like a raging river rushing over smooth stones, God's promise washed over David, echoed through the heavens, and went on and on, into forever.

Through the prophet Nathan, He told David that one day one of his royal sons would be…

A King like no other,
  defender and friend.
Always and forever,
  world without end!

But you'll never guess what happened next…

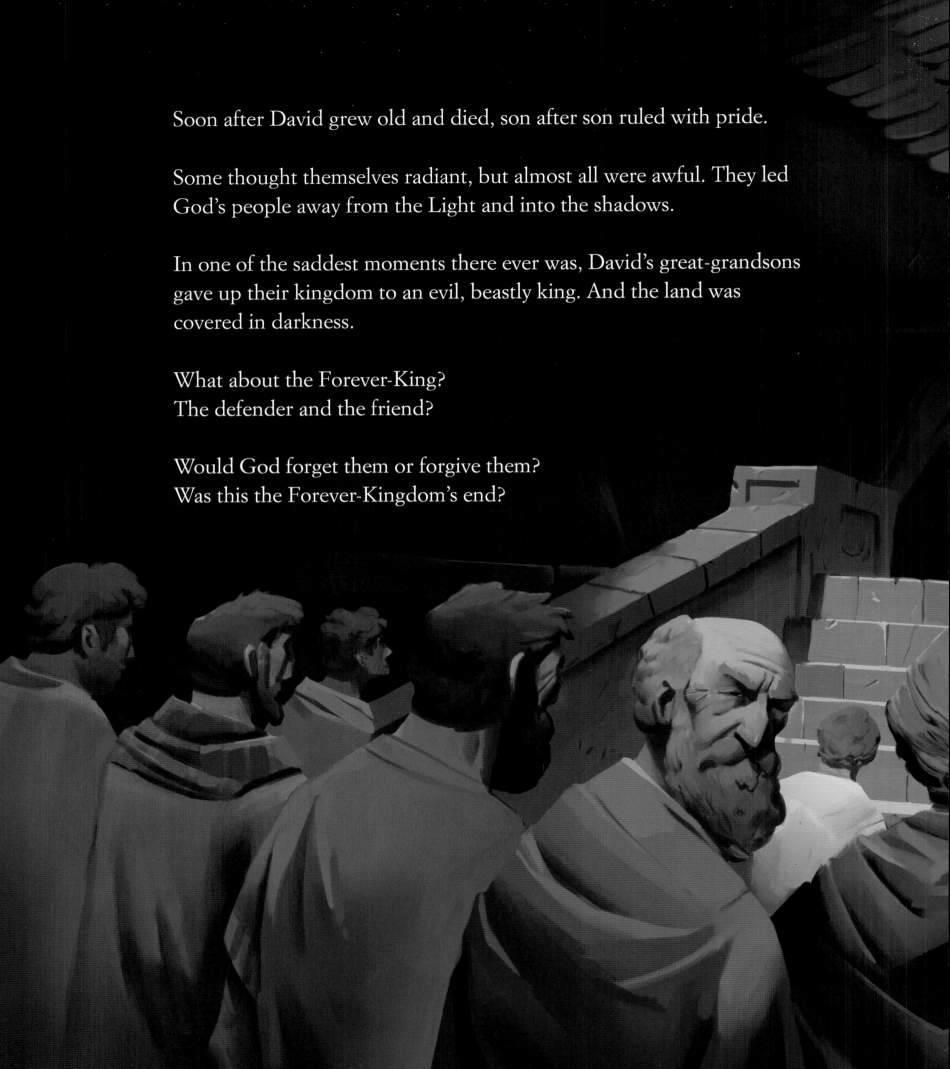

Soon after David grew old and died, son after son ruled with pride.

Some thought themselves radiant, but almost all were awful. They led God's people away from the Light and into the shadows.

In one of the saddest moments there ever was, David's great-grandsons gave up their kingdom to an evil, beastly king. And the land was covered in darkness.

What about the Forever-King?
The defender and the friend?

Would God forget them or forgive them?
Was this the Forever-Kingdom's end?

Like a long, cold night in the wilderness waiting for the dawn, God's people waited hundreds of years. God's promises seemed to fade into the shadows.

But those who knew God knew better.

A hush fell over God's heavenly host; they leaned in and listened carefully. This was the answer to the promises God made to Abraham and David, the moment they had all been waiting for!

At the perfect time, the High King of the Universe, the Creator of the Cosmos, the Great King of Old dispatched his armies of angels with a royal announcement!

With the light of seventy suns, the King's words lit up the night sky!

"It's David's Son! The Chosen One! The Defender and the Friend! Jesus! The Christ—the saving King—is born in Bethlehem!"

He announced His saving reign.

He dealt the enemy a fatal blow.

He put death to death, proclaiming,

"I am the King of kings!
Let all nations know!"

Can you guess what happened next?! The resurrected King was lifted up through the clouds right before His people's very eyes!

He rested on His throne
  at God's right hand in power.
Now all the angels praise Him
  every day and every hour!

He's a King like no other,
  defender and friend.
Always and forever,
  world without end!

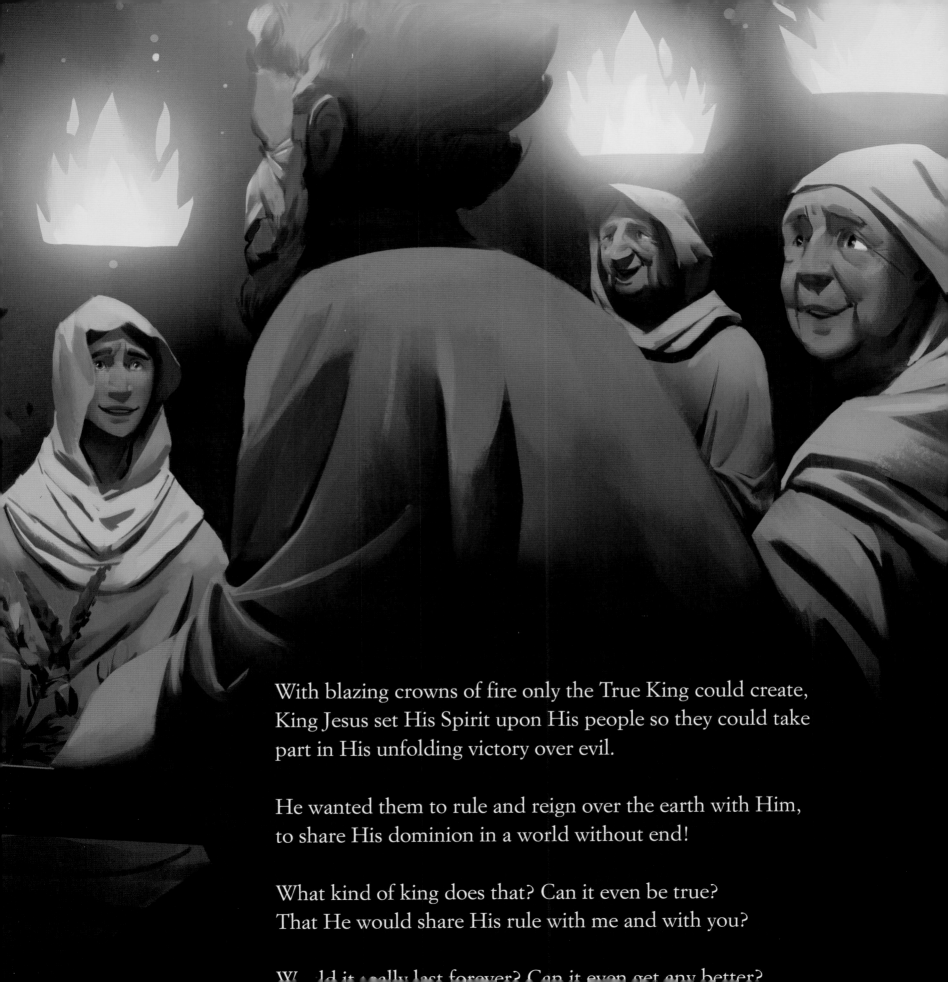

With blazing crowns of fire only the True King could create,
King Jesus set His Spirit upon His people so they could take
part in His unfolding victory over evil.

He wanted them to rule and reign over the earth with Him,
to share His dominion in a world without end!

What kind of king does that? Can it even be true?
That He would share His rule with me and with you?

Would it really last forever? Can it even get any better?

YES! It can!

Some day, at the perfect time, with the sound of a thousand trumpets, King Jesus will make His royal arrival!

With just a breath from His mouth, He'll conquer the Serpent-King for good!

With just a word from His lips, a Kingdom-City will burst forth—a shining city that only *this* King could create!

So much life and so much light will flow from the King's heart that the sun and the moon will fade into the brightness, and all the loyal followers of Jesus, from every tribe – tongue – and nation, will be united together in Him!

So we'll let our praise ring, and as one family sing!

"He's a King like no other,
  defender and friend.
Always and forever,
  world without end!"

As you can see, this is quite a different type of story, because this one is the true story of the whole world! And you, dear child of God, are living in the days of King Jesus when the Holy Spirit is turning His royal family into a loyal family!

So we give Him all our allegiance, loving Him with all our heart, soul, mind, and strength.

Our King reigns forever! Listen for His voice.

It may come gently like a quiet stream,
or like a raging river rushing over smooth stones.

It may come with the heat of a single flame,
or like seventy suns warming your bones.

But always know…

He's a King like no other,
  defender and friend.
Always and forever,
  world without end!

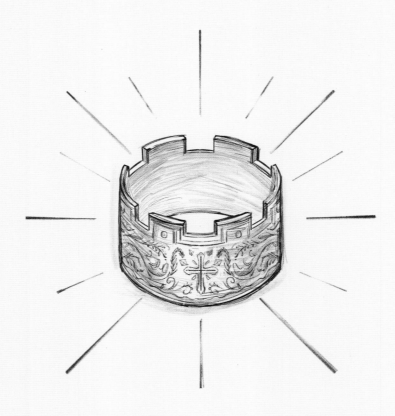

BIBLE REFERENCE GUIDE

Creation: *Genesis 1*

Image Bearers in the Garden of Eden: *Genesis 2*

Adam, Eve, & the Serpent-King: *Genesis 3:1-6*

The Flood: *Genesis 6-8*

A Promised Son (Abraham): *Genesis 17-18*

Bondage in Egypt: *Exodus 1:7-14*

The Exodus through the Sea: *Exodus 14:10-15:21*

The Giant & the Boy: *1 Samuel 17*

A Promised Son (David): *2 Samuel 7*

The Fall of the Kings & the Exile to Babylon: *2 Kings 24-25*

A Royal Announcement: *Luke 2:8-15*

The True King & His Saving Reign: *Mark 1:15 & Luke 8:1, 19:10*

The Triumphant King's Victorious Cross: *Luke 23:26-49 & John 15:12-27 & Colossians 2:14-15*

The Death of Death: *Luke 24:1-23 & Acts 2:24 & Romans 6:9*

The King's Great Commission: *Matthew 28:16-20*

The Enthronement of King Jesus: *Luke 24:50-53 & Acts 1:6-11, 2:29-36*

Image Bearers in the Upper Room: *Acts 2:1-11*

The Return of the King: *2 Thessalonians 2:8 & Revelation 19:11-16, 21-22*